Instant Expert: **Jesus**

D1026828

GHP

INSTANT
EXPERT

JESUS

→ Nick Page

LION

Published by Lion Books
an imprint of
Lion Hudson plc
Wilkinson House, Jordan Hill Road,
Oxford OX2 8DR, England
www.lionhudson.com/lion
ISBN 978 0 7459 5641 1
e-ISBN 978 0 7459 5796 8

First edition 2014

Acknowledgments
Scripture quotations are from The New Revised Standard
Version of the Bible copyright © 1989 by the Division of
Christian Education of the National Council of Churches in
the USA. Used by permission. All Rights Reserved.
Scripture quotations marked CEV are from the
Contemporary English Version New Testament © 1991, 1992,
1995 by American Bible Society, Used with permission.

A catalogue record for this book is available from the British
Library

Printed and bound in the UK, May 2014, LH26

CONTENTS

1. The Good News

"The beginning of the good news of Jesus Christ, the Son of God." (Mark 1:1)
It's a very odd thing, when you think about it, that a peasant worker from the fringes of the Roman Empire should turn out to be the most influential figure in human history.

Today, 2 billion people around the world claim to be followers of Jesus, and their number is growing every day.

The figure of Jesus – his sayings, the stories about him – dominate the cultural history of the West. His image fills our art galleries. His stories have influenced our language: we talk of good Samaritans, of the return of the prodigal son. Buildings built in his honour are found in towns and cities around the world. His name is even used as a swear word by those who would never call themselves believers.

Jesus' significance is not limited to Christianity. In Islam he is a prophet. Hindus and Buddhists find much in his teaching which resonates with their own practices. Gandhi, for example, was directly influenced by Jesus in his use of non-violent protest.

People from all races and social backgrounds identify with this man. Rich westerners in London and New York claim to follow him, as do peasant farmers in Colombia and factory workers in China. He is claimed as a capitalist by one side and a Marxist by the other.

So who was he? What is it about Jesus that inspires such fascination and devotion?

It is impossible, of course, in a book this size to summarize everything that has been written about Jesus. Even in the very earliest times, the writer of John's Gospel was aware that he had to leave out many other things that Jesus did. "… if every one of them were written down," he mused, "I suppose that the world itself could not contain the books that would be written" (John 21:25).

So, in this book I'm going to concentrate on the historical Jesus and the claims the early church made about him. These claims were made in four texts, four "biographies" of Jesus, which we call the Gospels.

The story of Jesus is told in four books within the Bible: the Gospels of Matthew, Mark, Luke, and John. It is difficult to classify these documents as there is nothing quite like them in any other ancient literature. Written in Greek, they are part biography, part record of Jesus' teaching, part interpretation of who Jesus was. The authors called this new type of writing *euangelion* – good news. In old English this was *gōd* ("good") and *spel* ("news"). Hence, gospel.

Most experts agree that Mark's account was the earliest of the four. Luke and Matthew use a lot of it in their own accounts (97 per cent of Mark appears in Matthew and 88 per cent in Luke) but they also contain extra teaching material and stories. These three Gospels cover most of the same events, in roughly the same order, using similar language.

The fourth Gospel, John, has a different structure and perspective and is unique in style. Although it shares many of the same events as the other Gospels, it also includes long speeches by Jesus and events which do not appear elsewhere. John's Gospel is very detailed in terms of chronology and shows that Jesus spent time in Jerusalem and went there for a number of festivals.

The early church attributed the Gospels to four different figures from early church history: Matthew, one of Jesus' disciples; Mark, a Jewish Christian from Jerusalem; Luke, an associate of Paul; and John, another of Jesus' disciples. They saw these four Gospels as the most reliable sources of information about Jesus' life. An early church leader called Justin, writing in the mid-second century AD, talks about "the memoirs ... which are called Gospels".

GNOSTIC GOSPELS

In recent years a lot of attention has been given to a group of writings known as the Gnostic Gospels. The earliest of these dates from the mid-second century, but most of them come from much later.

They were written to support the teaching and claims of various forms of mystical Christianity (Gnostic means hidden knowledge). They were written by Greeks, which is why Jesus is presented in them as detached from his Jewish background and portrayed as a Greek mystical philosopher. Some may contain nuggets of original material – the so-called Gospel of Thomas may contain some original sayings of Jesus – but on the whole they tell us a lot about what the Gnostics believed and nothing very much about the historical Jesus.

In recent years it has become fashionable to cast the Gospels as works of homage, if not downright fiction. But they claim something quite different. They claim to be eyewitness accounts. Here's the beginning of Luke's Gospel:

Since many have undertaken to set down an orderly account of the events that have been fulfilled among us, just as they were handed on to us by those who from the beginning were eyewitnesses and servants of the word, I too decided, after investigating everything carefully from the very first, to write an orderly account for you, most excellent Theophilus, so that you may know the truth concerning the things about which you have been instructed.

(Luke 1:1–4)

Luke claims to have created an ordered account – not the first, incidentally – from traditions passed down from eyewitnesses. And he is writing with a purpose: to persuade or reassure a high-ranking Roman, Theophilus, of the truth.

If we are going to explore the life of Jesus in any meaningful way, we have to work on the assumption that the Gospels are reliable sources. And, although hordes of scholars argue over what sayings of Jesus are original or not, whether he did the things attributed to him, or even who wrote the Gospels in the first place, the approach of this book is to assume that we are dealing with reliable testimony, gathered from different witnesses and arranged for one purpose: to give people good news.

And what is this good news?

It is that Jesus is the Son of God, who came to inaugurate a new kingdom on earth: the kingdom of God. This is what Christians believe about Jesus, and it is why the Gospels were written.

This is, perhaps, where we should start with Jesus. It is, after all, why he is so famous and influential. It is because the first followers believed him to be God. "Long ago God spoke to our ancestors in many and various ways by the prophets," says an early church letter called Hebrews, "but in these last days he has spoken to us by a Son, whom he appointed heir of all things, through whom he also created the worlds" (Hebrews 1:1–2). In John's Gospel it says,

"No one has ever seen God. It is God the only Son, who is close to the Father's heart, who has made him known" (John 1:18).

Now this is an astonishing and radical claim. And indeed, a highly dangerous one, because it put the teachings of Christianity on a direct collision course with a group of people who also saw themselves as gods: the Roman emperors.

2. Emperors, Kings, and Messiahs

"In those days a decree went out from Emperor Augustus that all the world should be registered." (Luke 2:1)

Jesus was born into a land under occupation. Judea had been conquered by the Romans in 63 BC.

Power was focused in the hands of a tiny ruling elite, at the top of which was the emperor. Rome reminded its subjects of their conquered status not only through routine acts of brutality, and the imposition of taxes and tariffs, but also through the propaganda of the imperial PR machine, which portrayed the emperor as a god.

Before his death in AD 14, Augustus composed an autobiography listing his triumphs and achievements. It was called *Res Gestae Divi Augusti: The Acts of the Divine Augustus.* Jews, of course, were rigidly monotheistic. For them, there was only one God and any other claim was blasphemy. But everywhere else in the empire there was a multitude of gods, and the Romans promoted a religious cult which viewed their emperors as divine. This language filled the official pronouncements about Augustus: in many places he is described as "the son of god", or "saviour of the world"; "the bringer of peace" or "the lord of all". An inscription from Preiene, written just a few years before the birth of Jesus, describes how providence sent Augustus as "a saviour" and states that "the birthday of the god Augustus was the beginning for the world of the good news that came by reason of him".

This is exactly the kind of language which Christians used about Jesus. So the claims that the Gospels make about Jesus are, in fact, more than startling or weird. They are seditious. Revolutionary. Every time that Christians said "Jesus is Lord" they were, in effect, saying "so Augustus isn't".

"In the days of King Herod of Judea..." (Luke 1:5)

Politically, the emperor might have been the ultimate power, but he was a long way away in Rome, and the Roman Province in which Jesus was born was overseen by the governor of Syria, who had his headquarters in Antioch. However, the Romans were great at delegation and they ruled their territories through client-kings, local rulers. At the time of Jesus' birth, the Romans were governing the country through Herod the Great. Herod came to power in 37 BC with the aid of the Romans, and he ruled for over thirty years. Herod was not Jewish, he was Idumean, from the region south of Palestine. Although he converted to Judaism, he was really only a nominal Jew.

Later, when Herod died, the kingdom was split between three of his sons: Archelaus, Antipater, and Philip. Archelaus only ruled for ten years before the Romans removed him for his excessive cruelty. They replaced him with a Roman military commander – a prefect. The prefect was based in Caesarea and he delegated government of Jerusalem and the surrounding area to the high priest and those who ran the Temple.

At the local level, the Romans and their client-kings employed a network of tax collectors to gather their revenue. Tax collectors purchased the rights to collect taxes, by guaranteeing their masters a certain amount of taxes and tolls. So they made profit by collecting as much as they could, by whatever means. Naturally, ordinary people hated the tax collectors, whom they viewed as collaborators and extortionists.

SAMARITANS

Between Jerusalem and Galilee was the region known as Samaria, the home of the Samaritans. The origins of the Samaritans are obscure. Jewish tradition held that these were the people who were settled in the area by the Assyrians many centuries before. Jews and Samaritans hated each other. The Samaritans, like the Jews, were monotheistic – they worshipped Yahweh, God of Israel. But they had their own, slightly different

theology and, crucially, their own temple on
Mount Gerizim.

"When shall we take them back?" asks a later
rabbi about the Samaritans. "When they renounce
Mount Gerizim and confess Jerusalem and the
resurrection of the dead."

The bulk of the populace in Palestine were peasants.
They might have some land on which they grew their
own produce, but life was hard. They had to pay taxes
to the Romans and tithes to the Temple, and if the
harvest failed they were in trouble. They might have
had to borrow money from the local tax collector, or
from the Temple, which served as a kind of central
bank. And then they had to hope for a bumper harvest
next year, because if they couldn't repay the loan, their
land was forfeit. And if you were a landless peasant
labourer, you were really poor. You relied on going to
the marketplace to find a job.

At the very bottom of society were those who had
nothing: beggars, widows, the dispossessed. If you
were blind or deaf or lame, if you had a skin disease, if
you had a demon, then you had no hope except to rely
on the generosity of others.

"... he was waiting expectantly for the kingdom of God." (Luke 23:51)

So, from the time of the prophets onwards, the Jews were almost constantly under the control of foreign powers. There was a brief period between the times of the Old and New Testament when they overthrew the yoke of their Greek overlords and gained some independence, but that ended in 63 BC when the Romans arrived and took over.

In such circumstances, Jews began to look to a deliverer. They believed that God would rescue them from oppression, just as he had all those centuries ago when he led them on the exodus from Egypt. And God would achieve this by sending a messiah.

Messiah is a Hebrew word which means "anointed one". The Greek word for "anointed" is *christos*, from which we get Christ. Different kinds of Judaisms had different opinions over what the messiah would be like. Theoretically, Jews expected two messianic figures: a king from the line of David and a high priest from the line of Aaron and Zadok. Some also expected a third figure: a prophet who would announce the arrival of the other two. But the main focus was on the king figure.

This king would drive out Israel's enemies, as his illustrious forebear David had driven out the Philistines. A psalm which was seen as a messianic prophecy said, "The Lord says to my lord, 'Sit at my right hand until I make your enemies your footstool'" (Psalm 110:1; see Luke 20:43). Victory in battle was non-negotiable: it was part of the messiah's job description.

The messiah was not a divine figure, but an anointed human being. He would bring in a new age of peace and prosperity. Most of all, the messiah would be a spectacular, high-profile success. He would not, for instance, be a peasant leader from the middle of nowhere who ended up being crucified by the Romans.

I mean, *as if*.

"Beware of the yeast of the Pharisees and Sadducees!" (Matthew 16:11)

Judaism in the first century was not one single, unified thing. The first-century Jewish historian Josephus, for example, talks about four types: the Sadducees, Pharisees, Essenes, and something he calls cryptically "the fourth way". And even within those groupings there were differences in theology.

The two main groups in Jesus' day were the Pharisees and the Sadducees. The Pharisees started as a grass-roots holiness movement. They were attempting to redefine Judaism in a way that actually helped those in the villages and small towns obey the Jewish religious law. So they built up a huge store of secondary legislation around things like Sabbath observance and the various Jewish purity laws.

The problem was that adding all these other clarifications and observations seemed to make life more complicated. This is Jesus' main criticism of them. The Pharisees believed that they were helping people to worship, but Jesus charged them with burdening people with more regulations.

Jesus had strong words for some Pharisees. He called them "whitewashed tombs" (Matthew 23:27) – they looked great but they were dead inside. However Jesus also had friends among the Pharisees. He is found eating in their houses in the Gospels (Luke 7:36; 11:37; 14:1). Some Pharisees, such as Nicodemus, even became disciples. They warned him when Antipas wanted to kill him (Luke 13:31).

The opponents of the Pharisees were the Sadducees. They were an urban elite, largely based in Jerusalem, with a particular following among the wealthy and the powerful. It is likely that the high priest and the ruling elite were Sadducees. Unlike the Pharisees, who drew on Jewish Scriptures such as the Psalms and the prophets, the Sadducees believed that only the Torah – the "Law", the first five books of the Jewish Scriptures – was authoritative. Josephus said that the Pharisees "had the multitude on their side" and "delivered to the people a great many observances by succession from their fathers, which are not written in the law of Moses; and for that reason it is that the Sadducees reject them…"

The Essenes were a more extreme, radical group. Some people think that the Qumran community, who hid the Dead Sea Scrolls, were Essenes, although none of the scrolls mention the word "Essene". They were a fundamentalist, ultra-purity group who lived in the towns and cities but kept themselves to themselves, which may be why they are not mentioned in the Gospels. The other group Josephus mentions – "the fourth way" – may equate to the Zealots. These were a religious-political group dedicated to armed rebellion against the Romans. Jesus' followers included a former zealot – Simon, "who was called the Zealot" (Luke 6:15).

"What is written in the law? What do you read there?" (Luke 10:26)

The Torah was, for all Judaisms, the bedrock of their belief. From this set of books – Genesis, Exodus, Leviticus, Numbers, and Deuteronomy – Jews drew their understanding of themselves as uniquely called, God's chosen people.

The Torah was behind all of the distinctive practices and beliefs of the Jews. In a world full of literally thousands of pagan gods, the Jews were monotheists. Why? Because the Torah told them to be so. Every day, devout Jews recited a prayer from the Torah: "Hear, O Israel: The Lord is our God, the Lord alone. You shall love the Lord your God with all your heart, and with all your soul, and with all your might" (Deuteronomy 6:4–5).

They observed the Sabbath. This was a uniquely Jewish custom. From sunset on Friday to sunset on Saturday no work was done. The time was set aside for the Sabbath meal, for going to synagogue and for resting from work. They followed Jewish purity legislation. To the Jews things were either pure or impure, there was no in-between. Jews – observant Jews – were pure; Gentiles were impure. Certain foods were clean, other kinds were unclean.

Jews were supposed to observe the pilgrimage festivals. Adult male Jews were expected to go to Jerusalem for the three main festivals: Passover, Pentecost, Tabernacles. While not everyone could do this, many made the effort to go at least once a year. (And talking of adult males, all male Jews were circumcised. Even those who converted to Judaism in later life.)

FESTIVALS

The three main festivals were Passover, Pentecost, and Tabernacles. All three were rooted in the Torah and, particularly, in the story of the exodus from Egypt, when God had rescued the Jews from slavery.

- Passover commemorated the escape from Egypt.
- Pentecost was a harvest festival, but was also associated with the giving of the law.
- Tabernacles was a commemoration of the time when the Israelites lived in tents in the wilderness.

There were extra festivals which were also significant, such as the Feast of Dedication (or Hanukkah) which celebrated the rededication of the Temple during the Maccabean revolt, when the Greek rulers of Judea were evicted, and Purim, which commemorated the story of Esther and the rescue of Jews from death in Persia. All of these festivals have a common theme: rescue, liberation, freedom. At festival times, Jews felt their occupied status keenly. No wonder that Josephus reported that it was at festival time that trouble tended to break out in Jerusalem.

"I have spoken openly to the world; I have always taught in synagogues and in the temple, where all the Jews come together." (John 18:20)

The study and interpretation of the Torah was one of the pillars of Jewish faith. The other pillar was the Temple. The Temple was the most important religious institution in the land. It was where sacrifices were made and festivals celebrated.

The building itself had been completely renovated by Herod the Great. He had built a massive raised platform constructed of gigantic blocks of stone. The retaining walls for this platform – known as Temple Mount – towered more than 80 feet above the surrounding roads and dominated the skyline of Jerusalem. On the platform stood the Temple itself – a magnificent building, made of cream-coloured stone and decorated with gold. The floor plan followed that of earlier temples, with the holy place, and the holy of holies – which was empty, of course, the ark being long since lost.

Within the Temple complex, different groups had different levels of access. Gentiles were allowed in the Court of Gentiles; women as far as the Court of Women; Jews as far as the knee-high wall at the north end of the Court of Israelites. The sanctuary, inside the Temple building, was the preserve of priests alone. And then, at the top of this pyramid of purity, there was the holy of holies, which only the high priest could enter, and only on one day a year: the Day of Atonement.

The Temple Mount itself was accessed by various gates. The south gates were reached by a wide flight of steps. To the north of the Temple stood the Antonia Fortress, the Roman garrison in Jerusalem. The fortress had been specifically designed and built to overlook the Temple, so that they could keep an eye on what was happening. The high priests' robes were stored there as a sign of the Jews' subjection to the Romans.

The activities of the Temple were run by a huge number of priests, Levites, and other functionaries. Some priests' positions were permanently attached to the Temple, but there were a large number of "part-time" priests living out in various communities who did Temple duty twice a year. John the Baptist's father, Zechariah, was one of these.

The high priest was the most coveted position. To attain it required personal wealth, since the high priest had to pay out of his own pocket for major sacrifices such as those on the Day of Atonement. But it brought significant income as well, since the Temple was an extremely wealthy institution. The Romans decided who would be high priest, and in Jesus' day the position was rotated among three or four of the ruling aristocratic families.

The dominant family was the house of Hanin. The first of the family to obtain the position was Ananus, son of Seth – or Annas, as he is called in the Gospels. His family was to dominate the post of high priest for the next sixty years. Annas was high priest from AD 6 to AD 15 and five of his sons were to hold the same office. Caiaphas, who was appointed in AD 18 was his son-in-law.

The high priest ruled with the aid of a council known as the Sanhedrin. This had representatives on it from different factions, including the Pharisees and the Sadducees.

The Temple was in Jerusalem. At the local level, people gathered together in synagogue. Indeed, that's what the word means: gathering. Not every place had a synagogue building; in some villages there was just a space to meet. Where a building was constructed it was simple. People sat in a "U" shape with the women segregated from the men. The synagogue was a place for prayer and study, but it was also where the community met to decide local issues.

The community was aided by scribes, who were local experts in the law. There were some high-status priestly scribes attached to the Temple but for most locally-based scribes, it was not a particularly high status job and many of them came from the poorer classes. Their job was to interpret the law for ordinary people and to read and write things such as contracts and agreements. It was thought honourable to support a scribe and some scribes apparently abused that, sponging off pious widows and eating them out of house and home.

In the synagogue, the Hebrew Scriptures had to be translated for most listeners. Hebrew was also the language of the liturgy chanted in the Temple, but most people couldn't understand it. Ordinary people spoke Aramaic. Jesus certainly did. Some of his sayings contain puns which only work in Aramaic, and in some places his original Aramaic words are preserved: *Talitha cum* ("Little girl, get up!") spoken to the little girl in Mark 5:41; *Ephphatha* ("be opened") spoken to the deaf man in Mark 7:34. He called Simon, *Cephas* – Aramaic for rock. Even on the cross, he cried out in Aramaic.

The other major language was Greek which, since the time of Alexander the Great, had been the shared language of the Mediterranean world. It was the language of trade and commerce – an international language, much as English is today. In the Temple an inscription warning Gentiles not to enter the inner courts was written in Greek. Then people also grabbed a few Latinisms – phrases from the language of occupation and the Roman military: prefect, mile, centurion.

3. The Birth of the King

"Where is the child who has been born king of the Jews?" (Matthew 2:1–2)

His real name is not Jesus. That's a Greek version, *Iesous*, a transliteration of his name. His Aramaic birth name was Yeshua, a short version of the name Joshua (in Hebrew Yehoshua). His parents would have called him Yeshu – the shortened, Galilean version of Yeshua. This was a very common name – the sixth most popular name among Jews of the time. The name Jesus sounds strange to us. But it is Joshua. Or Josh. Yeshu, the son of Yehosef and Miriam.

The story of his birth is, of course, one of the most famous stories in the world and the foundation of our Christmas celebrations. The early church, however, didn't consider it quite as important: the story only occurs in Luke and Matthew, and both writers include different details. They agree that Jesus' parents were called Mary and Joseph, that he was born in Bethlehem during the reign of Herod I (a.k.a. Herod the Great), that he ended up living in Nazareth, and that the birth had a whiff of scandal. Matthew states it simply: "… but before they lived together, [Mary] was found to be with child from the Holy Spirit" (Matthew 1:18). Luke has a more elaborate account, with an angel appearing to Mary and telling her that "The Holy Spirit will come upon you" and that the child "will be holy; he will be called Son of God" (Luke 1:35).

This, according to the Gospel accounts, is no ordinary baby.

INCARNATION

This is a key Christian idea about Jesus: that he was the incarnation of God. John wrote that "the Word became flesh and lived among us, and we have seen his glory, the glory as of a father's only son, full of grace and truth" (John 1:14). Incarnation means to appear in person, in the flesh. Christians claim – based on the Gospels – that God took human form and lived among us in the shape of Jesus. And this is reflected in another name which is applied to Jesus: Emmanuel, which means "God with us".

Some of the most familiar elements of the Christmas story are not actually in the Gospel accounts. The stable is never mentioned, and there's no inn, either. The word in Luke's account which is traditionally translated as "inn" actually means guest room, or spare room, or anywhere you might put visitors. In peasant homes of the times, the animals were brought indoors at night and the manger was in the lower section of the house. So the scenario that Luke paints is of a crowded peasant home where there was no room for a baby except for the animals' feeding trough.

Similarly, although we are familiar with the idea of three kings, the Bible never says that they were kings, or that there were three of them. Matthew's account talks of wise men – the word is *magi* – which indicates priests from the Persian empire in the east.

We don't know the exact date of his birth. Although in the West we celebrate it on 25 December, that date was not agreed upon until the fourth century AD. Earlier writers suggested November. Even the exact year is uncertain. We know from the Gospels that he was born during the reign of Augustus (Luke 2:1), that it took place while Herod was still alive, and that he was "about thirty" when he began his public work (Luke 3:23).

The date of Herod's death is generally agreed to be 4 BC. Jesus was born a little while before Herod's death, so it makes sense to assume that Jesus was born in late 5/early 4 BC. If Jesus' baptism took place in the autumn of AD 29, as some scholars have suggested, then he would have been thirty-two at the time. This fits pretty well with John's "about thirty" description. (You'll notice Jesus was actually born several years BC – before Christ! This is because the monk who invented BC and AD actually miscalculated the dates.)

Joseph and Mary were probably young: the usual age for a Jewish girl to be married was between thirteen and sixteen, and for boys not much older.

And they were poor. We know this because after Jesus'
birth, they go to the Temple and sacrifice two pigeons.
Pigeons were allowed as a sacrifice if you couldn't
afford a lamb or a goat. Also, when Mary hears of his
birth, she sings a song celebrating the triumph of the
poor and the humble. Known as *The Magnificat*, the
song celebrates the fact that God "has brought down
the powerful from their thrones, and lifted up the lowly;
he has filled the hungry with good things, and sent
the rich away empty" (Luke 1:52–53). This song makes
no sense at all unless Mary – and the man she was to
marry – was "lowly", poor, and even hungry.

According to Matthew, when Herod the Great found
out that there was a rumoured "prince" being born
in Bethlehem, he sent soldiers to kill the children.
Although some historians have questioned this event,
from what we know of Herod, such a thing is entirely
in fitting with his character. This was a man who
murdered two of his sons and one of his wives, who
ruled through terror, violence, and political cunning.

Matthew's Gospel records that Jesus escaped south,
into Egypt, returning when Herod died. When Joseph
and Mary returned, they discovered that Herod's
son Archelaus had inherited the southern part of the
kingdom. Archelaus was, if anything, more brutal than
his father. So they went back to Nazareth.

The area would have been devastated. In the
aftermath of Herod's death, his sons Archelaus and
Antipater went to Rome to argue over the terms of their
father's will. While they were away, disorder broke out

in Judea and Galilee. The Romans restored order by marching in and crushing the revolt. Thousands of Jews were taken as slaves in punishment, and most of the city of Sepphoris – only three miles from Nazareth – was destroyed. In Judea, the legate of Syria, P. Quintilius Varus had some two thousand rebels crucified.

So Jesus must have grown up surrounded by memories of violence and death, of families sold into slavery. His life was lived, like those of all citizens of occupied countries, against a background hum of fear.

"Is not this the carpenter, the son of Mary and brother of James and Joses and Judas and Simon, and are not his sisters here with us?" (Mark 6:3)

We know two things about Jesus' physical appearance: he was circumcised and he wore a fringed Jewish prayer shawl. He was, in other words, Jewish.

His father, Joseph, is described as a devout Jew – an upright or "righteous" man (Matthew 1:19). We know that Jesus went on pilgrimage to Jerusalem to observe the Passover (Luke 2:41) His parents circumcised him and had him named, and then, forty days after his birth, they took him to the Temple to be dedicated and for Mary's purification.

Nazareth was an insignificant place. Perched on a ridge above the surrounding countryside, it probably numbered not more than 400 people. There was nothing that we would recognize as a modern market economy. Instead, each household grew and consumed its own produce. In the shared family courtyard there would be an oven, a millstone for grinding wheat, and a cistern for storing water. The village provided a communal wine press and olive press. Families could be self-sufficient, owning a field, some sheep and goats, chickens, a donkey, and perhaps a cow. They would have olive and fruit trees: figs, pomegranates, and a vegetable garden for leeks, lentils, beans, peas, cucumbers, onions and garlic. Prosperity? Prosperity was owning your own vine.

Clothing was simple. Colours were a luxury. Most clothes were in muted colours, natural dyes. Men wore a *chiton* – a word which is often translated as "coat" but which is a basic undergarment, something nearer to what we would call a shirt. Later in life we know that Jesus had a tunic which was woven in one piece (John 19:23). On top of that they wore an oblong piece of cloth which served as a cloak in the daytime, and could be wrapped around as a blanket at night. For special occasions, or in richer families, you might wear a robe – a posher garment with sleeves. This was a sign of distinction. In Jesus' story of the prodigal son, the father dresses his son in a robe. This was tied with a sash or a belt. And they wore sandals on their feet.

Jesus grew up in a Jewish village. He attended synagogue, learned Hebrew, read the Torah. He lived among ordinary people living ordinary lives. And the farmers, the builders, the workshops, vineyards, and fishermen of Galilee all gave him the images with which he was to fill his stories of the kingdom of God.

Jesus was not an only child. He had four brothers and at least two sisters. His brothers were called James, Joses, Simon and Judas. (The word we translate as "James" is actually Jacob.) These are good, solid, Jewish names.

We can't be sure how much formal learning Jesus had. Formal education was rare and literacy rates throughout the ancient world were very low – that is why you needed scribes. We know that Jesus could read, but even though he was called rabbi – "teacher" – he does not appear to have had any formal training: later on, people were surprised at his learning. He would have learned the foundations of the Jewish faith, to recite the traditional prayers. As a devout man, Joseph may have encouraged his sons to learn at the synagogue and to study the Torah with the local scribe. Gifted children from well-off families might take their studies further and go to a rabbinical school, to sit at the feet of the teachers of the law. But Jesus never did this. Instead, when he became a man at thirteen years and a day, he took up his father's trade.

Although translated as "carpenter", the word used to describe Joseph, is *tekton*, which means someone who was also a general builder, a construction worker, including a stonemason and metalworker. A later writer, Justin Martyr, claimed that Jesus made ploughs and yokes (Justin was born in Samaria, so knew the region). It is likely, as well, that he and his father worked on the building sites in Sepphoris, since the city was being rebuilt by Antipas during those years.

The Roman Empire had ratified the will of Herod the Great and split the kingdom into four. Archelaus had control of Judea and Samaria, but proved so hideously inept that the Romans removed him from power and controlled the area through their own leader, a procurator, and the high priests in Jerusalem. Philip got Trachonitis and Batea; Antipas was called "tetrarch" – literally "ruler of one quarter of a kingdom" – and given the Perea and Galilee. The final part was known as the Decapolis: a federation of ten cities.

The fact that he was engaged in a manual trade, or even that he came from a poor background doesn't mean that Jesus was uneducated. Rabbis and sages of his day were not academics, but worked in a trade. Labour brought you some measure of independence. Shemaiah, a scribe from the generation before Jesus, said, "Love labour and hate mastery and seek not acquaintance with the ruling power."

Or, as the Jewish scholar Jacob Neusner's translation has it: "Love work, hate authority, don't get friendly with the government."

4. The Kingdom of God

"John the baptizer appeared in the wilderness, proclaiming a baptism of repentance for the forgiveness of sins." (Mark 1:4)

Mark's Gospel begins not with the birth of Jesus, but with John the Baptist – or John the Baptizer as he is sometimes known.

He is a fiery, Old Testament figure who dressed like the Old Testament prophet Elijah and baptized people in the wilderness. The key to John is what he wasn't. His father was a priest, he came from a priestly family, but John wasn't a priest. Instead he worked outside the religious structures, away from the Temple, calling people into the wilderness to repent. Only by repentance could Israel escape the coming wrath of the Lord.

John's disregard for the religious authorities becomes clear when we see that he baptized people who, in other fields, were beyond the pale. Prostitutes came to him. Tax collectors. Soldiers (and since Jews were exempt from military duty, these must have been Gentiles). We know as well that at one point he was baptizing in Samaritan country.

John was a truly radical figure who sometimes gets sidelined in Christian history. He prepared the way for Jesus, but we should not see him purely as some kind of warm-up act. John had a strong, urgent message of his own: repent. He called for repentance not only from ordinary people, but also from the ruling elite. Herod Antipas had eloped with the wife of one of his many stepbrothers. In John's eyes this constituted incest and thus made the ruler of Galilee impure.

Not, perhaps, the kind of thing a ruler wants to hear...

Sometime in AD 29, Jesus was baptized by John. This is one of the events in Jesus' life which all scholars agree to be genuine. Since his followers came to believe Jesus was without sin, the fact that he was baptized – an act of repentance for sin – would never have been invented by Christians.

So why was he baptized? Some see it as an act of solidarity with ordinary people. Others see it as signalling a new movement, a new period in his life. Baptism, after all, came to symbolize death and rebirth for Christians. Perhaps this was the death of Jesus' old life, with all its duties and obligations, and the beginning of something new. Others see it as confirmation: at Jesus' baptism, "... he saw the heavens torn apart and the Spirit descending like a dove on him. And a voice came from heaven, 'You are my Son, the Beloved; with you I am well pleased'" (Mark 1:10–11). It was a confirmation of who he was and what his purpose was.

After the baptism, though, Jesus was "driven out" by the Spirit into the wilderness. There he fasted for forty days, during which time he was tempted by Satan.

Satan means tester, accuser. And he tests Jesus in three specific ways. First he says, "If you are the Son of God, command this stone to become a loaf of bread" (Luke 4:3); then he promises that if Jesus worships him, he will hand Jesus authority over the cities of the earth; finally he tries to tempt Jesus to throw himself down from the high point of the Temple and call the angels to save him. Jesus is offered food to satisfy his hunger; he is offered worldly power; and the final temptation – to show everyone who he really was.

Jesus rejects all of the temptations, countering the devil's use of Scripture with Scriptures quotations of his own. And he returns from the wilderness having faced down the accuser.

Even then he does not set straight off into his mission. Instead he seems to have worked with John the Baptist for a while, baptizing in the southern Jordan while John moved into territory upstream.

This came to an end when Herod Antipas finally tired of John's invective against him. John was arrested, imprisoned, and eventually beheaded. The arrest seems to have been the trigger for Jesus to move back to Galilee and start his main mission.

"Now after John was arrested, Jesus came to Galilee, proclaiming the good news of God, and saying, 'The time is fulfilled, and the kingdom of God has come near; repent, and believe in the good news'" (Mark 1:14–15).

Jesus was not a politically neutral figure. He did not just go around "doing good". He was opposed by virtually every power group he met: Pharisees, Sadducees, Herodians, Temple authorities, scribes, and, of course, the Romans. Why would they do that, if all he was doing was "good deeds"?

The reason is that he was actually proclaiming something far more radical, more dangerous. He believed that his purpose was to bring in a new kingdom: the kingdom of God.

The arrival of the kingdom of God is the key message of Jesus' mission. The phrase "kingdom of God" (or Matthew's preferred alternative of "kingdom of heaven") occurs eighty-five times in the Gospels: thirty-seven in Matthew, fourteen in Mark, and thirty-two in Luke. John only uses the phrase twice, which might lead us to think that he was omitting something, but he uses an alternative phrase: "eternal life". (Actually Jesus uses this phrase in the other Gospels as well.) In John's Gospel, Jesus says, "I came that they may have life, and have it abundantly" (John 10:10). Abundant life is a hallmark of the kingdom of God.

This thread actually runs through the entire Bible. Although the phrase is never explicitly used in the

Old Testament, it frequently speaks of God as a king, reigning not only over Israel but over the whole world. It has been suggested that an alternative title for the whole Bible could be "the story of the coming of the kingdom of God".

Jesus wanted everyone to have access to God. To live in the kingdom of God was to accept the rule of God: the essence of a kingdom is that people there do the will of the king. Jesus taught his disciples to pray: "Your kingdom come. Your will be done, on earth as it is in heaven" (Matthew 6:10).

The kingdom of God on earth is where God's will is done.

THE LORD'S PRAYER

It is known as the Lord's Prayer, although that name was not given to it until the third century AD. It is really the disciples' prayer. It features in two forms in the Gospels: a longer form in Matthew and a shorter one in Luke. It also features in an early church discipleship manual called the Didache (which means teaching) showing that it was adopted as a significant, special prayer very early on. Tertullian, an early church writer, called it "the epitome of the whole gospel".

Jews believed in the kingdom of God, but that it would only come when the messiah expelled the Romans

and inaugurated a new golden age on the day of the
Lord. But Jesus said that the kingdom was not only
coming, it had already arrived. It was here, now, and
open to everyone. No one was excluded. In fact, the
lowest rungs of society were specifically welcomed
in. Beggars feature heavily in the Gospels. Widows
as well, and children. Then there are the lepers, the
demon-possessed. These are low status, powerless,
often outcast and marginalized individuals. Though
members of the aristocracy and the elite appear in the
Gospels, most of the cast is made up from the lowest
levels of society. The good news of Jesus was, above
all, good news for the poor. Jesus told them that God
cared for them and knew all about them. God, he said,
even knew the number of hairs on their heads.

The great Jewish story told how God chose his
people, rescued them, loved them, and would,
through them, eventually become the God of all the
nations. Jesus proclaimed himself the climax of that
story. The kingdom was here, the kingdom was active,
the kingdom was personal, and the kingdom had
room for everyone.

And that made the kingdom dangerous. In a
world ruled by the Romans and their client kings, to
advocate joining another kingdom was subversive
and seditious. Only the Romans could make someone
a king. It is worth noting that, when the Romans came
to execute Jesus, the charge sheet pinned above his
cross was the single title: King of the Jews.

"Now when Jesus heard that John had been arrested, he withdrew to Galilee. He left Nazareth and made his home in Capernaum by the lake..." (Matthew 4:12–13)

After John's arrest, Jesus went north to Galilee. He made his home in the fishing town of Capernaum, on the north shore of Lake Galilee. There he called his first disciples, Simon and Andrew, James and John. Jesus finds them fishing in Lake Galilee and calls them from their nets to become his disciples, promising them that from now on they will catch people, rather than fish. This was not the first time he had met them: according to John's Gospel, Jesus met them in Judea, when he was with John the Baptist. But now they left their nets and followed him.

DISCIPLES

Jesus called many people into discipleship. Disciple – the Greek word is *mathetes* – means apprentice, learner. Rabbis had disciples, small groups of students who learned by observing the rabbi and imitating him, and by discussing the Torah with him. Jesus adopts the same approach: his disciples were – and are – expected to imitate him, to be Christlike. Discipleship was an active commitment. Jesus called people to movement, to literally follow him. Fishermen left their nets; Levi the tax collector came out from his toll booth.

Jesus chose twelve core disciples. The number is symbolic, reminding Jews of the twelve tribes of Israel – Jesus' mission was for all Israel. The twelve included four fishermen, a tax collector, a zealot – a political radical. Some of them were relatives of Jesus (James and John were very likely his cousins). Some were married men. There was an inner circle of three: Peter, James, and John, who saw Jesus during some of his most crucial moments.

Along with them there was a much wider group of disciples. Jesus sent seventy of these on missions throughout Galilee. There were also "hidden" disciples, including Nicodemus in Jerusalem, and women – Mary Magdalene, and Joanna, wife of a high-ranking official at the court of Herod Antipas. Although they are never called "disciple", they did many of the same things that the men did. In one famous story, another Mary sits at Jesus' feet while he is speaking, much to the annoyance of her sister, Martha. This is often seen as a contrast between the contemplative life (Mary) and the active life (Martha), but Mary is actually adopting the classic pose of a rabbinic disciple and sitting at the feet of her rabbi. She is staking her claim to be a disciple. Mary, Martha, and their brother, Lazarus, also offered Jesus a place to stay. Jesus stayed with them at Bethany during the last week of his life, and may have made other visits there as well.

There are signs that the number of disciples declined in the latter part of his mission, when it was clear that he wasn't the type of messiah they thought he was going to be. Some fell away because the cost was too great.

Jesus' home in Capernaum was probably in the house of Simon and Andrew. In the ruins of Capernaum, archaeologists have found what they call "clan-dwellings", consisting of a central courtyard surrounded by a number of houses. Stairs within the courtyards allowed access to the roofs. The roofs were made of beams, covered with layers of packed mud – in one famous incident, the crowds around Jesus were so intense that some men climbed up to the roof, hacked through the mud, and lowered their invalid friend on a stretcher for Jesus to heal him. One of these houses was later converted into a church. It's a very good candidate for the house of Simon Peter in Galilee and the place which Jesus called home.

5. A Day in the Life of the King

There is an account in the first chapter of Mark's Gospel – echoed in Matthew and Luke – which shows a kind of "day in the life". This is the first time that Jesus comes to public notice, and it is a kind of microcosm of all his work. It contains many of the elements that were to make him famous: teaching, exorcisms, healing, sharing meals, the adulation of the crowds, and his blatant disregard for religious convention. It gives an insight into why people found him so compelling, so intriguing, so attractive, so irresponsible, and even so infuriating.

"They were astounded at his teaching, for he taught them as one having authority, and not as the scribes." (Mark 1:22)
It starts on the Sabbath. Jesus goes to the synagogue in Capernaum where he begins teaching. People are amazed by the power and authority of his words.

Jesus was a brilliant – and highly unorthodox – teacher. He had no formal training and, although some of his teaching took place in synagogues, Jesus often taught on the move: walking around Galilee. A lot of teaching happened in fields, in a boat, on the side of a hill, in houses – wherever he found himself. And everywhere, people were astonished at the power and authority of his words.

The authority of Jesus' teaching is a recurrent theme in the Gospels. There was something about the way in which he taught that was different. Typically, teaching of the time drew attention to previous teachers and "authorities", piling up references and quotations, or rabbinic teaching, which dissected the Torah in forensic detail through question and answer. Jesus both asked and answered questions, and he did provoke debate. But he did not teach in this kind of detailed manner, nor did he bother much about precedent, or even scriptural authority. His teaching seems to claim a power and authority of its own.

In one way, though, Jesus' teaching echoes that of the rabbis: he expects people to copy him. During John's account of the Last Supper, Jesus strips and washes the disciples' feet as a demonstration of how they should serve one another. He says: "So if I, your Lord and Teacher, have washed your feet, you also ought to wash one another's feet. For I have set you an example, that you also should do as I have done to you" (John 13:14–15).

A lot of Jesus' teaching involves provocative statements, or questions. He encourages questions. He uses clever forms of speech: metaphors, analogies, stories. He uses paradox: "...those who want to save their life will lose it, and those who lose their life for my sake, and for the sake of the gospel, will save it"; "Whoever wants to be first must be last" (Mark 8:35; 9:35).

He uses humour and exaggeration. He gives
people nicknames which sum up their characteristics.
Most of all he fills his teaching with examples from
everyday life. And many of these examples turn up
in Jesus' most characteristic form of teaching, which
were the sharp, disturbing, disruptive stories that we
call parables.

**"With many such parables he spoke the word
to them, as they were able to hear it; he did
not speak to them except in parables, but
he explained everything in private to his
disciples." (Mark 4:33–34)**
There are some forty parables in the Gospels (the
difficulty in being precise is because sometimes
it's hard to define what is a parable and what isn't).
Some are little more than one-liners. Others are
longer, more complex narratives. They are intended
to be memorable as hardly anyone in his audience
could read. Everything was heard and carefully
remembered.

These were not fairy stories or children's tales.
They were stories intended to make the abstract
real, to ground the kingdom of God in the everyday
world of the listeners. They were intended to engage
the audience – and at times to enrage them as well.
Sometimes they were simple and clear, at other times
baffling and provocative. But they all made people think.

Jesus was not unique in telling parables: other
rabbis did the same. But Jesus' parables were earthier.

God appears in many guises: landowner, father, obstinate judge; whereas in rabbinic parables God is nearly always a royal figure.

Indeed, that's what parables are: they are stories about the kingdom of God. They are not direct comparisons or allegories. The king in the story of the talents might represent God, but that doesn't mean that God necessarily behaves like the king in that story. Everything depends on the point that Jesus is trying to make.

MAJOR PARABLES OF JESUS

Parable	Matthew	Mark	Luke
The Sower	13:1–9, 18–23	4:1–9, 13–20	8:4–8, 11–15
The Weeds	13:24–30, 36–43	4:26–29	
The Mustard Seed	13:31–32	4:30–32	13:18–19
The Yeast	13:33		13:20–21
The Hidden Treasure	13:44		
The Valuable Pearl	13:45–46		

Parable	Matthew	Mark	Luke
The Net	13:47–50		
The Lost Sheep	18:10–14		15:3–7
The Unforgiving Servant	18:23–35		
The Two Sons	21:28–32		
The Tenants	21:33–44	12:1–11	20:9–18
The Wedding Feast	22:1–14		14:16–24
The Ten Bridesmaids	25:1–13		
The Talents	25:14–30		19:11–27
The Good Samaritan			10:29–37
The Rich Fool			12:16–21
The Barren Fig Tree			13:6–9
The Wedding Feast			14:7–11
The Lost Coin			15:8–10
The Prodigal Son			15:11–32

Parable	Matthew	Mark	Luke
The Dishonest Manager			16:1–9
The Rich Man and Lazarus			16:19–31
The Persistent Widow			18:1–8
The Pharisee and the Tax Collector			18:9–14

"He commands even the unclean spirits, and they obey him." (Mark 1:27)

Back to that Sabbath in Capernaum. In the synagogue is a man possessed by a spirit. His presence is a surprise: from a Jewish point of view, demons defiled a person, which is why this man is described as having an "unclean spirit". Such people were ostracized and certainly not admitted to the synagogue. Nevertheless, there he is: perhaps he is an intruder, an interloper. Whatever the case, the spirit in him cries out against Jesus. Jesus replies: "Be silent, and come out of him!" The unclean spirit leaves the man, throwing him into convulsions "and crying with a loud voice" (Mark 1:25–26).

Our modern world finds demon possession baffling and even abhorrent. It is the stuff of horror movies. And, indeed, in the Gospels there is something horrible about it. What is portrayed in the Gospels is sometimes very close to mental illness: for instance, the account of the boy repeatedly self-harming (Mark 9:22), or people chained because of violent behaviour would fit with certain diagnoses of psychotic behaviour. At other times it is more clearly supernatural, such as the casting out of Legion – the many demons that inhabited the man in Gerasa (Mark 5:1–20). Demon possessed people were not viewed by others as inherently evil: they were innocent victims, in the power of something that they could not control.

Ancient cultures took it for granted that evil powers could inhabit people, and they tried to combat this in many ways: through spells, incantations, herbal remedies, special rings, and amulets. Jewish exorcists were common, and pagan magicians offered similar "services" through charms and amulets. But Jesus differed in a number of ways.

First, he performed these deeds in his own power. No charms. No incantations. No amulets. He just told the demon to shut up and get out. The Greek word often used is *ekballo*, from *ballo* – to throw. Jesus literally chucked them out.

Secondly, he restored people to wholeness. Jesus' exorcisms were acts of liberation and release. To have a demon was to be unclean. These people were exiled to the margins, living outside the towns or even in graveyards. So, in casting out their demon, Jesus brought them back into their community. Released from this terrible powerless slavery, they were now free to live their lives as they wished, and to rejoin their community.

Thirdly, Jesus explicitly linked the exorcism with the arrival of the kingdom. For Jesus, defeating these powers was a sign of the kingdom of God: "If it is by the finger of God that I cast out the demons, then the kingdom of God has come to you" (Luke 11:20).

The casting out of demons was a crucial part of Jesus' ministry, and exorcisms make up the single biggest category of healing in Matthew, Mark, and Luke. Even his enemies acknowledged Jesus performed such miracles, although they claimed that he did it because he was in league with the devil.

We are not comfortable in our rational, scientific age with the idea of miracles, but the Gospel stories about Jesus give us no choice. There are too many stories for them all to be invented, and they are woven too closely into the account of his life. Jesus – the historical Jesus – performed miracles. That is why he was remembered. It has been popular, in certain circles, to "de-mythologize" Jesus, to remove the miraculous with the hope that it will leave us the historical Jesus. What it actually leaves us with is the forgettable Jesus. Without the miraculous there is no reason why Jesus should have been remembered by his followers.

Certainly the miraculous exorcism in the Capernaum synagogue makes Jesus famous. News starts to spread throughout Galilee. But he wasn't doing it for effect. It was done to help a man in need. And as a result the man is made whole, restored, not just to his full faculties, but to the whole community.

"And all in the crowd were trying to touch him, for power came out from him and healed all of them." (Luke 6:19)
This is followed by another, different kind of healing. From the synagogue meeting, Jesus goes to Simon's house where he heals Simon's mother-in-law, sick with a fever.

So, after the first exorcism comes the first physical healing. And this act brings the crowds flocking to Jesus' door. Mark tells us that at sundown – which marks the beginning of the day after the Sabbath – people bring their sick and possessed to Jesus for healing and exorcism (Mark 1:32–34).

Like the exorcisms, the healing miracles are acts of restoration. There is more to them than simply "making someone well". The lame, the blind, the deaf were reduced to begging: that was the only work they could do. So when Jesus healed them it was like a whole new life: he restored their dignity and their capacity to earn and to support themselves and a family.

Jesus healed those who were excluded. The classic examples of this were people with leprosy. This is not what the modern world calls leprosy – which is Hansen's disease – it covers a range of skin diseases, skin rashes, blemishes or other kinds of disfigurements. While not fatal, these diseases were seen as rendering the sufferer impure. Even being under the same roof as a leper made you impure; lying or eating within the house would necessitate a complete change of clothes (Leviticus 14:33–47).

Lepers were therefore kept in a state of near-permanent quarantine and excluded from towns and communities. The lepers Jesus encounters on the edge of a village in Samaria shout at him from a distance (Luke 17:12). These people were barred from the Temple: the place most connected with the earthly presence of God. Recovered lepers could enter, but even then there was a special place in the Temple – the House of Lepers – where they would have to undergo various purification rituals. It didn't mean that God did not care for them. But it did mean that they could never fully engage with the worshipping community. Jesus changed all that.

Jesus is recorded as touching lepers *before* they were cured (Matthew 8:3; Mark 1:41; Luke 5:13). This touch makes Jesus himself impure, but it doesn't seem to worry him. So when Jesus heals a leper he is doing more than ridding someone of a skin disease. He is making the impure, pure. The exiled, the forgotten, the "dead" are brought back to life.

The healings are acts of restoration. But they are also, sometimes, acts of deliberate provocation. Strictly speaking, healing was one of the thirty-nine categories of prohibited work in the rabbinical teachings on the Sabbath. Jesus was always getting into trouble for breaking the Sabbath rules in one

way or another, or for contravening Jewish food laws
and purity rules. On the Sabbath he healed people
of serious, but not fatal, conditions. It was, reasonably
enough, permitted to heal or rescue someone in a
life-threatening condition on the Sabbath, but lesser
conditions could wait until the next day. The same is
true of his disciples who plucked grain to eat as they
walked through a field on the Sabbath. They were not
starving to death, they could have avoided the "work"
of plucking grain, but they didn't. Jesus' response
was a plea to put things into proper perspective. The
Sabbath was a gift to people, not a cage in which to
imprison them (Matthew 12:1–8).

The healings, then, say something about who
Jesus is and the authority that he has. They were
proclamations of the arrival of the kingdom of God
and the messianic status of Jesus. From prison, John
sends disciples to find out whether Jesus really is who
John thought he was. Jesus replies, "Go and tell John
what you hear and see: the blind receive their sight,
the lame walk, the lepers are cleansed, the deaf hear,
the dead are raised, and the poor have good news
brought to them" (Matthew 11:2–5).

JOHN'S SIGNS

In John's Gospel, Jesus performs a series of what
John calls "signs". These are miracles which show
who Jesus really is. The miracles which John
explicitly identifies as signs are:

- Changing water into wine in Cana (John 2:1–11)
- Healing the royal official's son in Capernaum (John 4:46–54)
- Healing the paralytic at Bethesda (John 5:1–18)
- Feeding the 5,000 (John 6:5–14)
- Healing the blind man (John 9:1–7)
- Raising Lazarus from the dead (John 11:1–45)

Some add Jesus walking on water (John 6:16–24) to this list, but John doesn't call it a sign.

John sees all these as signs which point to Jesus' true nature and purpose. All of them are to do with abundant life.

Jesus performed these miracles first and foremost because he felt compassion. He was genuinely upset by the suffering he encountered. When he sees the harassed, exhausted crowd, when he meets a leper excluded from society, when he is greeted by blind men, when he goes to Nain and meets a widow who has lost her only son, when he drives out the demon at the foot of the mountain, the Gospels use the rather wonderful Greek word *splanchnizomai*. This is translated as "to have pity" or "feel sympathy", but the root of the word comes from *splanchnon* which meant the inward parts – the guts of an animal or human. Jesus is gutted. He is stomach-wrenchingly moved.

He feels this especially in Bethany, when he arrives to find his friend Lazarus has died. Jesus is so upset, he weeps. Why? It's not because of loss – he raises Lazarus from the dead. He's weeping because the pain and the grief are just so wrong. He feels it deeply. And he calls Lazarus out of the tomb.

Along with the healings and the exorcisms, there are other miracles which are hard to quantify. Jesus feeds thousands of people with just a few loaves and some fish. He walks on water. He calms a storm. The important thing about these miracles is not their extent. Raising someone from the dead seems more impressive than healing a blind man, but both are extraordinary, unexpected acts of power. The important thing about these miracles is that they, once again, point to who Jesus is. "Your way was through the sea, your path, through the mighty waters," wrote the psalmist (Psalm 77:19). In the Old Testament it was God who walked on water. In the Old Testament it is God who brings resurrection of the dead. And now Jesus is doing it.

You don't think…

"And after he had dismissed the crowds, he went up the mountain by himself to pray." (Matthew 14:23)

After the events in Capernaum, we are told that "In the morning, while it was still very dark, he got up and went out to a deserted place, and there he prayed" (Mark 1:35). Throughout his mission, the pressure was

on Jesus. He was faced with unremitting pressure from
the authorities – who opposed what he was doing;
from people who brought him endless questions; and
from people who were always wanting to be healed.
In such circumstances Jesus' personal practice was to
seek what solitude he could. At key moments in his life
he retreated, escaping into the wilderness.

Everything that Jesus did was fuelled by his
relationship with God and, in particular, with his deep,
radical, and persistent prayer. Jesus spoke a lot about
prayer. He told stories which showed the need to
persist, and to pray with faith and belief. "I tell you,
if you have faith the size of a mustard seed," he said,
"you will say to this mountain, 'Move from here to
there', and it will move; and nothing will be impossible
for you" (Matthew 17:20).

And the most startling aspect of his prayer life was
that it portrayed a closer, much more personal God.
The Jews did not use the name of God: they substituted
it with other words, such as "the Lord". But when Jesus
talked about God, he used the Aramaic word *abba* –
the deeply personal, Aramaic name for father.

We should not think necessarily of modern fathers.
The father in the ancient world was an authoritarian
figure who had control over his family. So this is not
some completely indulgent father, but neither is it
a father to be scared of. Instead it is someone who
combines both love and authority.

This is a unique aspect of Jesus' teaching. In hardly
any other sources from this period is God addressed

in this way. The Aramaic word *abba* became so important to the early church that they adopted it, even though they all spoke Greek. Luke's version of the Lord's Prayer preserves the Aramaic feel of the original: "When you pray, say: Father..." (Luke 11:2).

If God was their father, then they were all part of his family. At one point, Jesus' mother and brothers arrived to take him home – they thought he was out of control. He rejected them, looking around at the crowd and saying, "Here are my mother and my brothers! Whoever does the will of God is my brother and sister and mother" (Mark 3:34–35). This was a shockingly radical statement in the first-century world, where your kin, your family, was everything. But Jesus' followers went on to adopt this vocabulary themselves. They talked of each other as brother and sister. Jesus was the elder brother; they were a new family.

Jesus goes out "throughout Galilee, proclaiming the message in their synagogues and casting out demons" (Mark 1:39). Matthew's version has Jesus "proclaiming the good news of the kingdom and curing every disease and every sickness among the people" (Matthew 4:23). This, then, was the message: healing, casting out demons, and telling people the good news of the kingdom.

6. The Royal Banquet

"For John the Baptist has come eating no bread and drinking no wine, and you say, 'He has a demon'; the Son of Man has come eating and drinking, and you say, 'Look, a glutton and a drunkard, a friend of tax-collectors and sinners!'" (Luke 7:33–34)

One of the symbols associated with the arrival of the messiah was a banquet. The idea comes from Isaiah 25:6, where the prophet says, "On this mountain the Lord of hosts will make for all peoples a feast of rich food, a feast of well-matured wines...". Jesus was clearly a big fan of this idea. He told stories in which the messianic banquet featured. He miraculously fed thousands of people. And he shared meals with people. A lot.

Eating with his disciples – and others – was one of the most characteristic activities of Jesus. Indeed, his opponents accused him of having far too good a time. John fasted and preached a radical self-discipline in repentance and preparation. Jesus just enjoyed a party.

It was not just the party that people found so outrageous, it was also the guests, the company that Jesus kept. Jesus ate with tax collectors. Jewish custom

said that even to stick your head into the house of a
tax collector made you unclean. To be a tax collector
was, politically and socially, to collaborate with the
Romans. Tax collectors had to bid for the franchise.
They promised the Romans a certain amount of taxes
and tolls. Anything above their contractually agreed
amount they had to gain themselves. Extortion and
corruption was rife. These were not people who sinned
accidentally. Yet Jesus ate with them, challenged them,
welcomed them into the kingdom of God.

He certainly demanded that they should reform
their lives. But he was happy to share a meal with
them *before* that reform happened. Sharing a meal
was a significant act in first-century culture. It meant
acceptance. It meant that you were inside the circle,
that you were OK. So the eating and drinking has a
serious purpose. It says to the outsiders: "You are part
of the family, part of the kingdom." It was a meal which
offered a side-order of love and acceptance.

The meal was so important that it became a focal
point of early church activity. One of the most striking
things about the early church was that they ate together
– people of all races and social classes. It was a radical
equality. And it all stemmed from their founder.

At one meal, Jesus is sitting in the house of a
Pharisee named Simon, when a woman enters. She
starts to wash his feet with her tears and dry them with
her hair. Then she pours ointment over his feet. This is
an astonishingly sexual act for the time, and the host
is scandalized. He believes that it proves how unholy

Jesus is. But the woman lived in that world. That was the only language she had. Jesus understood that she was using the only vocabulary she had available. He rebukes his host:

> ... *I entered your house; you gave me no water for my feet, but she has bathed my feet with her tears and dried them with her hair. ... her sins, which were many, have been forgiven; hence she has shown great love. But the one to whom little is forgiven, loves little.*
> **(Luke 7:44–48)**

Jesus' relationship with women was one of the things which shocked people. In the culture of the time a woman had no legal status and hardly any rights. She was there to cook and clean, give birth, raise children. In public she was covered. And yet in the Gospels women feature time and time again; some in quite scandalous situations. Jesus' followers not only included wives and mothers, but prostitutes and foreigners – people with whom no "respectable" Jewish male would associate.

John tells the story of Jesus meeting with a Samaritan woman at a well (John 4). For any male Jew, talking to a woman alone was taboo. Yet here a male Jew asks a Samaritan woman to pass him a cup of water. All Samaritan women were deemed unclean by orthodox Jews. So Jesus is willing to risk impurity in order to talk to her. Further, this woman has a reputation; we discover that she has had five husbands

and she is now living with another man. So in all
kinds of ways – socially, culturally, religiously – this is
a shocking, taboo-busting conversation, but it ends
with the woman realizing that Jesus is the messiah
and running into town to bring everyone to see this
remarkable man.

In Jesus, women found someone who would talk to
them, view them with respect. And they understand
him better, perhaps, than many of the men. In Bethany,
Mary anoints him for burial, intuitively understanding
what his fate will be. Her sister, Martha, says to Jesus,
"Yes, Lord, I believe that you are the Messiah, the Son
of God, the one coming into the world" (John 11:27).

In Simon the Pharisee's house, Jesus says to the
woman who anointed his feet: "Your sins are forgiven"
(Luke 7:48). This, too, was immensely outrageous.

> *For which is easier, to say, "Your sins are forgiven", or
> to say, "Stand up and walk"? But so that you may know
> that the Son of Man has authority on earth to forgive
> sins" – he then said to the paralytic – "Stand up, take
> your bed and go to your home."*
> **Matthew 9:5–6**

When people brought a paralyzed man before Jesus,
he said, "Son, your sins are forgiven." The Jewish
scribes were outraged. They knew that only God had
the authority to forgive sins. It was not so much that
Jesus himself was doing the forgiving, it was that he
seemed to know with absolute certainty what God

thought about it. He believed that he had "authority on earth to forgive sins" (Mark 2:5,10), and the proof of this authority lay in the miracles that he performed.

In statements and stories, through deeds and actions, Jesus kept implying that he was more than a mere mortal. He told a story in which he likened Israel to tenants in a vineyard. The vineyard owner sends a series of men to collect the rent but the tenants beat and even kill them. Finally the owner sends his own son. And the tenants kill him as well. The message of the story was clear. The vineyard was a common Old Testament symbol for Israel: "... the vineyard of the Lord of hosts is the house of Israel," wrote Isaiah, "and the people of Judah are his pleasant planting" (Isaiah 5:7). Jesus implies that he is the son of the owner – and that he will be killed. No wonder that when he told this story, in the Temple, the authorities were so angry they wanted to arrest him (Mark 12:12).

In John's Gospel we see Jesus as the obedient son of the father, who has come to show people what God is like. John, as we've seen, portrays Jesus at the start of his Gospel as the eternally present "word" of God. But he also describes Jesus using seven "I am" sayings, metaphors which describe him and his purpose. The key thing here, though, is that the phrase "I am" was also one of the names of God. At one point, Jesus says "before Abraham was, I am!" (John 8:58). This is not just a muddle up of tenses, it is a claim to be God, and Jews recognized it as such: they tried to kill him for blasphemy.

THE "I AM" STATEMENTS IN JOHN

The metaphorical "I am" statements made by Jesus are:

1. I am the bread of life 6:35, 48, 51
2. I am the light of the world 8:12; 9:5
3. I am the gate for the sheep 10:7, 9
4. I am the good shepherd 10:11, 14
5. I am the resurrection and the life 11:25
6. I am the way, the truth, and the life 14:6
7. I am the true vine 15:1

"In everything do to others as you would have them do to you; for this is the law and the prophets." (Matthew 7:12)

Another cause of outrage was Jesus' attitude to the law. Jesus didn't reject the Torah, but nor did he accept it wholesale. In fact he reimagined it, sometimes in startling new ways.

In one Q&A session, a legal expert asked Jesus which of the 613 commandments in the Torah was the most important. Jesus answered:

The first is, "Hear, O Israel: the Lord our God, the Lord is one; you shall love the Lord your God with all your heart, and with all your soul, and with all your mind, and with all your strength." The second is this, "You

shall love your neighbour as yourself." There is no other commandment greater than these.
Mark 12:29–31

The first was a common answer; it is the Jewish prayer known as the *shema* and it was recited every day by devout Jews. But the second comes from an entirely different section of the Torah: Leviticus 19:18. Jesus combines them, summing up the entire law in a handful of words. It starts with complete devotion to God. And out of that flows love for your neighbour.

But Jesus goes on to expand on the concept of who is our neighbour, and he does it through one of his most explosive and well-known stories: the tale of the Good Samaritan (Luke 10:25–37). The tale relies on the notorious hatred between Samaritans and Jews. In the story a Jew is attacked by robbers and left for dead. Along the road come a priest and a Levite, who both ignore the man's plight. Instead, he is helped by a Samaritan – viewed as a heretical apostate by the Jews – who pays for all his care. In the end it is the Samaritan who has acted as a neighbour.

What is missed in this story is that both of the men who ignored the Samaritan are attached to the Temple: the first was a priest there, the second a Temple worker. They avoid the man because in Jewish law if you touched a corpse you would be impure (Numbers 19:13). Jesus implies that it was possible to interpret the Torah in an unimpeachably orthodox way, and in doing so entirely miss the point of what obeying God is all about.

Perhaps Jesus' most radical interpretation of the Torah is in the large chunk of teaching known as the Sermon on the Mount. Like the Lord's Prayer, the Sermon on the Mount was not called that, originally. The title was given to it by St Augustine in the fourth century. The truth is that it is not a sermon. (Nor, indeed, was it delivered on much of a mount.)

What it is, is a collection of Jesus' teaching brought together in Matthew's Gospel. (In Luke's Gospel the same material is spread throughout the text.) It starts with a statement about who is most important, most blessed in the kingdom of God. Not the wealthy or the healthy – the traditional view of the signs of God's blessing – but the poor. Those who mourn. Those who hunger for justice and who struggle for peace. It is, in fact, the very people who thought that God could never care about them.

In a section known as the "antitheses", Jesus first repeats the traditional, Torah-based view, and then goes on to expand it:

> *You have heard that it was said … "You shall not murder"; and "whoever murders shall be liable to judgement." But I say to you that if you are angry with a brother or sister, you will be liable to judgement …*
>
> *You have heard that it was said, "You shall not commit adultery." But I say to you that everyone who looks at a woman with lust has already committed adultery with her in his heart.*
>
> **Matthew 5:21–22, 27–28**

It isn't enough, for Jesus, to just not commit murder or adultery: you have to deal with the murderous and adulterous thoughts in your heart. This is taking the Torah to a much deeper, more demanding, interior level. And then Jesus says something truly startling:

> *You have heard that it was said, "An eye for an eye and a tooth for a tooth." But I say to you, Do not resist an evildoer. But if anyone strikes you on the right cheek, turn the other also ... You have heard that it was said, "You shall love your neighbour and hate your enemy." But I say to you, Love your enemies and pray for those who persecute you, so that you may be children of your Father in heaven ...*
> **Matthew 5:38–39, 43–45**

Love your enemies? Do not retaliate? The law allowed "An eye for an eye and a tooth for a tooth" but Jesus was telling his disciples not to fight. This was one of his most revolutionary teachings: non-violence. In fact I'd go so far as to suggest that Jesus invented the concept of non-violence. He was not saying, "Do nothing." He was not saying, "Do not stand up to injustice." He was recognizing that those who meet violence with violence get sucked in to a spiral. He had seen it enough in Jewish history, the way that liberators become the oppressors.

What Jesus' policy of non-violence achieved was two-fold. First, it forced the oppressors to recognize what they were doing. A person who strikes you on the cheek – and then has to do it again – has to at least think about what they are doing. Secondly, it transfers power away from the oppressor: "... if anyone forces you to go one mile, go also the second mile", said Jesus (Matthew 5:41). "To go the extra mile" has become proverbial for putting extra effort in to helping someone. In fact, it's a much more revolutionary act. In the Roman Empire, soldiers could forcibly conscript foreign nationals to carry loads for up to one mile. Jesus is suggesting that you obey the command – and then keep going. They think they have forced you to do something: but you take back your will. It suddenly becomes not their choice, but yours.

> *... whoever wishes to become great among you must be your servant, and whoever wishes to be first among you must be slave of all.*
> **Mark 10:43–44**

Jesus modelled a revolutionary form of leadership. In the final months before he entered Jerusalem, he was approached by James and John with a request: they wanted to sit at his right and left hand when he came into his glory. In Matthew's Gospel it is not just the brothers, but also their mother who made the request (Matthew 20:21), most probably all three were involved.

It's likely that their mother is Salome, the sister of Mary (Matthew 27:55; Mark 15:40; John 19:25). So they were family. They had the idea that family – kin – would be rewarded in the messianic kingdom of Jesus. They have profoundly misjudged both Jesus and the nature of the kingdom of God. They know how the ruling class operates and they think that the new kingdom will be the same. To sit at the right and left hand of a ruler was to sit in the highest places of honour.

But Jesus turns all their expectations upside down. His followers are not to lead in the same way as the Gentile rulers, who love to lord it over each other. Instead, whoever wants to lead in his kingdom will be like a slave. "For who is greater," asked Jesus, "the one who is at the table or the one who serves? Is it not the one at the table? But I am among you as one who serves" (Luke 22:27). The Greek word indicating the servant here is *diakonos*. It's significant that when the early church came to name the officials who looked after their churches they chose one of the words used here: they became "deacons". They became servants.

The request of James and John shows that they believed he was the messiah. But it also shows that even his closest disciples misunderstood the nature of his messiahship. People believed he was the kind of messiah they were expecting: the military one who would kick out the Romans and put the Jews back in charge.

One of the most notable features of the Gospels is that Jesus constantly rejects the title of messiah or, at least, refuses to allow himself to be defined by it. Sometimes he tells people not to publicly call him the messiah. When Peter and Martha and people like that call him the "Christ" he does not reject or deny the title, but he tells them to be quiet. He hardly ever uses the title himself, or even mentions it.

Even when he was arrested, at his trial, he remained opaque. In Matthew and Luke's accounts of the trial, when asked if he was the messiah, he replied, "You say that I am." Only in Mark does he give a straightforward answer: "I am."

So what is behind this? Mainly it is to do with the expectations. He knew that he was not the kind of messiah they were expecting. And he refused to be confined by their expectations. They were looking for the great revolution, the anointed figure that would lead his people out of bondage and defeat the enemy.

Jesus did that. But the enemy he defeated was not the enemy they were anticipating. And the liberation he offered was far, far deeper than they had ever dreamed.

7. The Death of the King

"Look, your king is coming to you, humble, and mounted on a donkey, and on a colt, the foal of a donkey." (Matthew 21:5; quoting Zechariah 9:9)

After the years spent in Galilee, Jesus makes his way to Jerusalem. It is clear that this is going to be the climactic moment. He is aware of the fate he must suffer. At certain points the disciples try to talk him out of it. But he rebukes them and they continue on their way.

They arrive in Jerusalem in time for Passover. The year is probably AD 33, although some scholars opt for AD 30. Jerusalem is packed with pilgrims ready to celebrate the festival. And when he gets to Jerusalem, Jesus makes an overt statement of his messianic status. But he makes it through the manner of his entry into the city.

He enters Jerusalem riding on a donkey, in the manner which echoed that predicted by Zechariah for the messiah. His appearance causes a sensation. Crowds gather to cheer him into the city. They lay their cloaks on the ground and wave palm leaves – the usual greeting for a king. This is what Christians celebrate every year as Palm Sunday.

After that he heads straight into the Temple to make trouble. Many of Jesus' parables contain subtle – and not so subtle – criticisms of the Temple aristocracy. But it was his so-called "cleansing" of the Temple which really brought things to a head and determined the Temple authorities to get rid of him.

The Temple precincts contained stallholders who exchanged money and sold animals. All male Jews had to pay a Temple tax, and they had to pay this in a specific kind of currency: the Tyrian shekel. The Temple leadership made money on this venture. The animal sellers in the sanctuary provided animals for people to sacrifice. But at festival times, when there were a huge number of people in Jerusalem, the prices went up. There is also evidence that the aristocratic families who ran the Temple were making money from these activities.

Jesus certainly believed that the people who ran the Temple, the high priestly families, were abusing their power. And he marched into the Temple courtyard and overturned the tables of the moneychangers and drove the traders out. Jesus was not against the activities of the Temple, as such. If he had been opposed to sacrifice he would have stopped it in the central courts where the sacrifices took place. What he was opposing was the way that people were profiteering from the desire of pilgrims to engage in worship.

The Temple was a place which had a complicated relationship with money and power. It was not just a place of worship; the Temple police (some 7,000 of them) acted as the security force for Jerusalem. The Temple owned large amounts of land, from which it gathered significant revenue. It used this revenue to lend money to people, like a bank. The money was guaranteed against property. So if the people couldn't pay, the Temple foreclosed on their property. How do you think it got all that land in the first place? When the Temple authorities were ousted in the first days of the Jewish revolt, one of the first things the rebels did was to burn the list of people who owed money to the Temple.

Jesus' attack on the Temple traders must have sealed his fate in the eyes of the authorities. But they could not arrest him because the crowds were highly supportive of him. So they bided their time and looked to build up a case against him. That case was greatly helped by Jesus' inflammatory statements about the future of the Temple.

When his disciples admired the building, he told them starkly: "You see all these, do you not? Truly I tell you, not one stone will be left here upon another; all will be thrown down" (Matthew 24:2). He talks about the time of destruction that is coming. The rising tide of zealous anti-Roman nationalism among the Jews can only have one outcome: the Temple, this symbol of Israel, would be destroyed. You can imagine how his words would have been reported.

But Jesus also talked of more mystical events. He said that he would return one day in judgment. He used a kind of heightened poetic language, known as apocalyptic, to talk of the day of the Lord. Stars will fall. The sun and moon will go dark. And one day Jesus will return. In the meantime he urged his disciples to be prepared. He will arrive like a thief in the night. And then this:

> When Jesus had finished saying all these things, he said to his disciples, "You know that after two days the Passover is coming, and the Son of Man will be handed over to be crucified."
>
> **Matthew 26:1–2**

"They wanted to arrest him, but they feared the crowds, because they regarded him as a prophet." (Matthew 21:46)

Why did people want him dead? Well, most of them didn't. Most Jews in Jerusalem at that time were on Jesus' side. The Temple authorities could not arrest Jesus for most of the week, because it would have caused a riot. In the end, they arrested him while he was alone, and then executed the sentence before most of the people could find out about it.

For the Jewish authorities he was an irritation and a potential revolutionary. He had made blasphemous statements. He had threatened the Temple. He disturbed the status quo. For the Romans, they didn't care one way or the other. Jesus was a nobody. He became a bargaining chip for Pilate who gained increased cooperation from the Jews and staved off a potential riot.

Jesus, on the other hand, not only predicted his death, he saw it as absolutely vital. He knew it would happen. He told his disciples that the Son of Man had to die. It was inevitable, even necessary. He knew it would trigger something: "For as the lightning flashes and lights up the sky from one side to the other, so will the Son of Man be in his day. But first he must endure much suffering and be rejected by this generation" (Luke 17:24–25).

Jesus saw the mysterious passages in Isaiah which talk of the suffering servant as predicting his own death (Isaiah 52:15 – 53:12). He believed that his death would be the culmination of a life of selfless giving. He talked about it in terms of a rescue act: "… the Son of Man came not to be served but to serve, and to give his life a ransom for many" (Mark 10:45).

Somehow, then, Jesus saw his death as bringing liberation. We are reminded again of that fundamental Jewish story, the exodus from Egypt. In the meal that he shared with his disciples the night before his arrest, he made the connection even more explicit.

It is known as the "Last Supper" and appears not only in all four Gospels but also in the apostle Paul's first letter to the church at Corinth, which is probably the earliest account:

For I received from the Lord what I also handed on to you, that the Lord Jesus on the night when he was betrayed took a loaf of bread, and when he had given thanks, he broke it and said, "This is my body that is for you. Do this in remembrance of me." In the same way he took the cup also, after supper, saying, "This cup is the new covenant in my blood. Do this, as often

as you drink it, in remembrance of me." For as often as
you eat this bread and drink the cup, you proclaim the
Lord's death until he comes.
1 Corinthians 11:23–26

In context, this is yet another taboo-busting statement
by Jesus. The Torah made it clear that Jews were
forbidden to drink blood, which was seen as the life
of the animal. Jesus seems to be indicating that this
celebration brings life, through his death.

We are not sure if it was really a Passover meal.
Although it shares some elements of the traditional
Passover, there is no lamb, or unleavened bread, which
are *the* core ingredients of a Passover meal.

But perhaps the key connection with Passover is
the symbolism. Jesus becomes the Passover lamb. The
wine is his blood, the bread is his broken body. He
told his disciples to "Eat this as a way of remembering
me" (Luke 22:19, CEV).

LORD'S SUPPER

The early church instituted a celebration called
Eucharist, which means "thanksgiving", otherwise
known as the "Lord's Supper". This was part of a
shared meal to which all the Christian community
were invited, rich or poor. This surrounding meal
was known as the agape meal, or "love feast".
During this meal the wine and the bread were

shared. So the meal was a symbol of Christ's death, and also a symbol of the new community which he had brought into being.

"Then the chief priests accused him of many things." (Mark 15:3)

After the meal, Jesus and the disciples went out to a garden called Gethsemane, to pray. Gethsemane is outside the walls of Jerusalem, and only a few hundred metres from the road to Jericho. Jesus could have escaped but chose to stay. And there he was arrested, his location betrayed to the authorities by one of his own disciples – Judas Iscariot – who later bitterly regretted his actions.

During the night, Jesus faced a series of "trials". He was taken before the old high priest, Annas, founder of the dynasty in charge. Then he was dragged before the religious leaders and the council of the Temple. This was a highly charged emotional affair: Jesus was spat upon and beaten.

In the end it was decided that he must die. But there was a problem. The Jewish authorities were not allowed to execute anyone: only the Romans reserved the right to do that. So early the next morning the Temple authorities sent Jesus across to Pilate, the prefect. The charges brought before the Romans were incitement to riot, urging non-payment of taxes, and claiming to be the king (Luke 23:1–2).

Pilate was in town because it was festival time. Normally he lived in Caesarea, which was on the coast and had temples, a theatre, and a stadium – all the amenities of a sophisticated Greco-Roman city. But at festival time he had to come into Jerusalem to hand over the high priest's robes and make sure that no riots broke out in the tense, crowded atmosphere.

And that was the key motivating force behind Pilate's decision. He found nothing wrong with Jesus and offered his release to a rent-a-mob gathered together by the Temple authorities. But they demanded his death.

The charges in the Jewish hearings were blasphemy. In the end, keen to keep the peace and fearful of a Jewish riot, Pilate agreed. Jesus was brutally beaten, mocked and humiliated, and sent out to be crucified.

"It was nine o'clock in the morning when they crucified him." (Mark 15:25)

Jesus was executed as a foreign insurrectionist: the sign over his cross said "King of the Jews".

Cicero described crucifixion as a "cruel and frightful sentence". It was designed to humiliate and terrify. And it was reserved for the lowest criminals – slaves, bandits, and rebels. It has been called an act of imperial terror. There were millions of slaves in the Roman world and they had to be kept under control. Many cities in the empire had highly visible crucifixion sites in order to frighten slaves into obedient submission.

Criminals would carry their heavy crossbeam to the site and there they were nailed to the beam, which was then set on an upright pole. Horrific as it was, crucifixion didn't actually kill you. Instead, victims died of blood loss, exhaustion or heart failure. Jesus probably died of massive blood loss, caused by the beating he took before the sentence was carried out. He was already too weak to carry his crossbeam.

SAYINGS FROM THE CROSS

The different Gospels record different things that Jesus said whilst on the cross. Together, they are known as the seven sayings on the cross.

1. Jesus prays for forgiveness for his executioners: "Father, forgive them; for they do not know what they are doing" (Luke 23:34).

2. One thief mocks him, the other recognizes that Jesus is innocent. Jesus says to the latter, "Truly I tell you, today you will be with me in Paradise" (Luke 23:43).

3. Jesus asks the "beloved disciple" to look after his mother: "Woman, here is your son... Here is your mother" (John 19:26–27).

4. Jesus cries "I am thirsty" and is given only sour, vinegary wine to drink (John 19:28–29).

5. Jesus quotes Psalm 22 in Aramaic: *"Eli, Eli, lema sabachthani?"* – "My God, my God, why have you forsaken me?" (Matthew 27:46; Mark 15:34)

6. Jesus' last words as recorded in Luke: "Father, into your hands I commend my spirit" (Luke 23:46).

7. Jesus' last words as recorded in John: "It is finished" (John 19:30).

At the moment of Jesus' death there were strange, cosmic events: the earth shook and rocks split (Matthew 27:51) and darkness filled the sky (Luke 23:44). According to the Gospel writers, the curtain in the Temple, guarding the holy of holies, was torn in two from top to bottom (Matthew 27:51; Mark 15:38; Luke 23:45). In Matthew, the earth opened and dead men walked around (Matthew 27:52–53).

Standing near the cross were the women who supported Jesus, and the author of John's Gospel. Jesus' Galilean disciples were, understandably, in hiding.

According to the Gospel accounts, his body was taken down from the cross and buried in a borrowed tomb, belonging to Joseph of Arimathea, a wealthy supporter of Jesus. The women went with the burial party to see Jesus put into the tomb.

And that was that. Another wannabe messiah dealt with.

8. The Return of the King

"Why do you look for the living among the dead? He is not here, but has risen."
(Luke 24:5)

He was put in the tomb on Friday, just before sunset. On the Sunday morning, just after sunrise, some women went to the tomb to anoint his body. His burial had been so hurried due to the Sabbath that they had not been able to perform the task properly.

And when they got to the tomb they found...

Well, the accounts, as recorded in the Gospels, differ in some details: Matthew has two women going to the tomb; Mark, three; Luke at least five and John only one. The stone is already removed in three of the Gospels: in Matthew an angel rolls it aside as the women arrive. Mark and Matthew have one angel, Luke and John have two. But the angels tell the women: "He is not here, but has risen!" (Luke 24:5).

We could argue about the discrepancies, but that would be to ignore the main issue, the elephant in the tomb, as it were. Because all the stories agree that the tomb was empty and Jesus was no longer there. He had risen from the dead.

Looking across the stories, we can piece together
a kind of composite account. The women, including
Mary Magdalene, go to the tomb early in the morning
and find it empty, the stone rolled back, and the
grave clothes on the floor. Angels appear and tell the
women that Jesus has risen. The women go and tell the
other disciples, after which Peter and John come and
investigate for themselves.

Then there are the meetings. In the garden, Mary
Magdalene meets Jesus (whom she thinks is the
gardener). Walking on the road away from Jerusalem,
two disciples find themselves accompanied by a
stranger. They talk about the unusual events: "Some of
those who were with us went to the tomb and found it
just as the women had said; but they did not see him"
(Luke 24:24). The stranger takes them through the
Scriptures explaining to them why Jesus had to die.
They invite him to share a meal with them and when
he breaks the bread they realize who he is. They rush
back to Jerusalem and find that Jesus has appeared to
Simon Peter. And then Jesus appears to them all.

So we have four different resurrection appearances
on that day: to Mary, Peter, the two disciples on the
road, and the other disciples in the upper room.
Subsequently Jesus appears to Thomas, to the
disciples in Galilee, and to many others.

All the Gospels except Mark tell stories about
Jesus' resurrection – and that is probably because
the original ending of Mark is missing. In fact, like
the Last Supper, the earliest collection of Jesus'

resurrection appearances comes from Paul's letter to the Corinthians where he says that Christ

> *appeared to Cephas, then to the twelve. Then he appeared to more than five hundred brothers and sisters at one time, most of whom are still alive, though some have died. Then he appeared to James, then to all the apostles. Last of all, as to one untimely born, he appeared also to me.*
>
> **1 Corinthians 15:5–8**

Note that Paul says that some of these people are still alive and can still be consulted.

So what are we to make of this? And what about those differences in the accounts?

Well, the obvious answer is that is what you get in eyewitness accounts – especially where people are witnessing extreme events. In fact, you could argue that it reinforces the truth of the event. If all this was fabricated, then it is more likely that the discrepancies would be smoothed out, or that one story would be preferred above the others. But the early church did not iron out the inconsistencies; instead, it chose to keep the different stories, because they wanted to honour the testimonies of real people. That was what the people saw.

And then there are the women. In the first-century world, if you were inventing a story, you would not choose women for your witnesses. Women had no legal standing. Their testimony was worthless in a court. They were emotional, irrational, unreliable witnesses.

Then there is the fact that there was never any counter-argument. No one ever argued that the tomb wasn't empty, although they argued as to what the cause of that was.

And the claim itself was strange. Many Jews believed in the resurrection of the dead, but they saw it as something happening at the end, at the day of judgment. It was not going to arrive way ahead of time and on an individual basis.

The accounts are very simple and matter of fact. They do not try to introduce any symbolism. They are not told in the style of a visionary experience. Indeed, there is an emphasis on the physicality of the body. Jesus offers to let Thomas touch him. In one resurrection appearance he eats fish. In another he cooks fish – a breakfast on the beach for the disciples who are out fishing. His body is changed: Mary Magdalene and some other disciples did not immediately recognize him, but it is a real body.

So this is not some "spiritual" resurrection. And the church continued to emphasize these two key factors: the empty tomb and the visible, resurrected man. You need both. If you only have the empty tomb then we are talking about deception or grave robbing. And if Jesus appeared but the tomb was not empty, then he was a ghost or a hallucination.

But the two together – well, for the followers of Jesus it meant that he was back. And that life had suddenly changed completely. And that, perhaps, is a final piece of corroboration, because something turned this dispirited, frightened, disillusioned bunch of people into powerful, highly motivated, completely committed witnesses to the story of Jesus. They, at least, were utterly convinced that Jesus had risen. And their conviction and faith spread like wildfire through the city of Jerusalem and beyond.

9. The People of the Kingdom

"Go therefore and make disciples of all nations, baptizing them in the name of the Father and of the Son and of the Holy Spirit, and teaching them to obey everything that I have commanded you. And remember, I am with you always, to the end of the age." (Matthew 28:19–20)

At first the followers of Jesus were called "Nazarenes". And they called their distinctive set of beliefs and practices "the Way".

In the beginning, they were based in Jerusalem, and they were all Jews. The core group were those who had been disciples of Jesus before his death, many of whom had seen the risen Jesus after his resurrection, but many others were added to their number. These early Christian communities met to pray together, to study the Hebrew Scriptures, to look after the poor, and to share their memories of Jesus' teaching. One of the ways they did this was through the shared meal which they called the *Eucharist* ("thanksgiving"). They were doing what Jesus asked them to do the night before his death: eat bread and drink wine and remember his sacrifice for them.

Their fundamental beliefs were that Jesus was the messiah, that God had raised him from the dead, and that he had ascended to heaven from where he ruled with God. Jesus was no longer with them physically – in his place he sent the Holy Spirit. He would return one day to complete the arrival of the kingdom of God on earth. In the meantime, they were to make more and more disciples.

From the start, as far as we can tell, they viewed Jesus as divine. They believed he was the Son of God. To know Jesus was to know God. To obey Jesus, worship Jesus, pray to Jesus was to obey, worship and pray to God. And through Jesus, they were now sons and daughters of God.

This was a radical departure. Jews were sternly monotheistic. The idea of a group of Jews just casually starting to worship Jesus is impossible. Something happened to completely change their view of who he was. That something was the resurrection of Jesus and the power of the Holy Spirit in the lives of the believers.

His death on the cross was an example of his love for others. It was a defeat for the powers of oppression and darkness. But more than that, it was a sacrifice on behalf of others. The early church preached that Jesus died in the place of sinners: that sinners deserve death, but that Jesus has paid the price. And through his resurrection we can have new life. Forgiveness from sins and fullness of life: those are the two suns around which the Christian life orbits.

We can see this very early on. This is not some later teaching, it is a seam which runs right through the heart of the Gospels. Paul talks about it in his letter to the Philippians, where he quotes from an early Christian statement of belief. It describes Jesus, who

> *though he was in the form of God, did not regard equality with God as something to be exploited, but emptied himself, taking the form of a slave, being born in human likeness. And being found in human form, he humbled himself and became obedient to the point of death – even death on a cross.*
>
> *Therefore God also highly exalted him and gave him the name that is above every name, so that at the name of Jesus every knee should bend, in heaven and on earth and under the earth, and every tongue should confess that Jesus Christ is Lord, to the glory of God the Father.*
>
> **Philippians 2:6–11**

This, then, summarizes what the first followers believed about Jesus, and what forms the core of Christian belief even today. Jesus was God who became man. He lived on earth and was executed by the authorities. But he rose again and is now reigning in heaven with God. The man that they thought was Jesus of Nazareth turned out to be Jesus Christ, Son of God.

And the kingdom which he came to bring started to spread. It went into Samaria and Syria, across to North Africa, overseas to Cyprus, to Asia Minor, Macedonia, Greece, Rome... it was on the move.

And it has been moving outwards ever since.

In fact it was outside the borders of Palestine, in Antioch in Syria, around AD 44, that the followers of Jesus first acquired their distinctive name. The people of Antioch were known for their scurrilous wit and invention of nicknames. And they turned their mockery onto this new group of people, with their allegiance to "Christ" and their insistence on serving one another. They called them the *Christiani*. It's a mash-up of two words: the Greek word *Christos*, meaning "anointed one" and *Chrēstos*, which means "good" or "useful" and which was a common slaves' name.

And they have been Christians ever since.

FURTHER READING

Of course, the best thing to do if you want to find out more about Jesus is to read the four Gospels.

Otherwise, here is a list of books which contain a wealth of fascinating insights into the life and times and teaching of Jesus.

General background

Karen Armstrong, *A History of Jerusalem: One City, Three Faiths*, London: HarperCollins, 1997.

Peter Connolly, *Living in the Time of Jesus of Nazareth*, Oxford: Oxford University Press, 1983.

Herbert Danby, *The Mishnah, Translated from the Hebrew*, London: Oxford University Press, 1933.

Martin Goodman, *Rome and Jerusalem: The Clash of Ancient Civilizations*, London: Penguin, 2008.

Richard A. Horsley, with John S. Hanson, *Bandits, Prophets, and Messiahs: Popular Movements in the Time of Jesus*, San Francisco: Harper & Row, 1988.

Joachim Jeremias, *Jerusalem in the Time of Jesus: An Investigation into Economic and Social Conditions During the New Testament Period*, London: SCM, 1974.

Jacob Neusner, *The Mishnah: A New Translation*, New Haven: Yale University Press, 1988.

John Wilkinson, *Jerusalem as Jesus Knew It: Archaeology as Evidence*, London: Thames and Hudson, 1978.

Gospels and commentaries

Richard Bauckham, *Jesus and the Eyewitnesses: The Gospels as Eyewitness Testimony*, Grand Rapids: Eerdmans, 2006.

George R. Beasley-Murray, *John*, Waco: Word Books, 1987.

Raymond Edward Brown, *The Birth of the Messiah*, New York: Doubleday, 1993.

Raymond Edward Brown, *The Death of the Messiah*, London: Geoffrey Chapman, 1994.

Joseph A. Fitzmyer, *The Gospel According to Luke*, 2 vols: New York; London: Doubleday, 1981,1985.

Robert Horton Gundry, *Mark: A Commentary on His Apology for the Cross*, Grand Rapids: Eerdmans, 1993.

Craig S. Keener, *The Gospel of John: A Commentary*, Peabody: Hendrickson Publishers, 2003.

Craig S. Keener, *The Gospel of Matthew: A Socio-Rhetorical Commentary*, Grand Rapids: Eerdmans, 2009.

Ched Myers, *Binding the Strong Man: A Political Reading of Mark's Story of Jesus*, Maryknoll: Orbis, 2008.

Historical Jesus

Kenneth E. Bailey, *Jesus Through Middle Eastern Eyes: Cultural Studies in the Gospels*, London: SPCK, 2008.

James D. G. Dunn, *Beginning From Jerusalem*, Grand Rapids: Eerdmans, 2008.

Craig S. Keener, *The Historical Jesus of the Gospels*, Grand Rapids: Eerdmans, 2009.

David Flusser, with R. Steven Notley, *The Sage From Galilee: Rediscovering Jesus' Genius*, Cambridge: Eerdmans, 2007.

Martin Hengel, *Crucifixion in the Ancient World and the Folly of the Message of the Cross*, London: SCM, 1977.

Michael R. Licona, *The Resurrection of Jesus*, Nottingham: Apollos, 2010.

Bruce J. Malina, *The Social World of Jesus and the Gospels*, London: Routledge, 1996.

John P. Meier, *A Marginal Jew: Rethinking the Historical Jesus*, London: Doubleday, 1991.

Jerome Murphy-O'Connor, *Jesus and Paul: Parallel Lives*, Collegeville: Liturgical Press, 2007.

Nick Page, *The Longest Week: What Really Happened During Jesus' Final Days*, London: Hodder & Stoughton, 2009.

Nick Page, *The Wrong Messiah: The Real Story of Jesus of Nazareth*, London: Hodder & Stoughton, 2011.

Nick Page, *The One-Stop Bible Atlas*, Oxford: Lion Hudson, 2010.

E. P. Sanders, *Jesus and Judaism*, London: SCM, 1985.

Gerd Theissen, and Annette Merz, *The Historical Jesus: A Comprehensive Guide*, London: SCM Press, 1998.

Géza Vermès, *The Changing Faces of Jesus*, London: Penguin, 2000.

N. T. Wright, *Jesus and the Victory of God*, London: SPCK, 1996.

N. T. Wright, *The Resurrection of the Son of God*, London: SPCK, 2003.

John Howard Yoder, *The Politics of Jesus: Vicit Agnus Noster*, Grand Rapids: Eerdmans, 1972.

Other sources

Talmud, Tractate Kutim 28, page 16

Tertullian, *Concerning Prayer* 1, page 39

Justin Martyr, *First Apology*, 66, page 3

Josephus, *Antiquities* 18.23–24, page 19

Shemaiah, Mishnah Avot 1.10, page 34